This House Hunting Journal Belongs To:

ADDRESS *Information*

PREVIOUS ADDRESS:

REALTOR:

NAME:
AGENCY:
PHONE:
EMAIL:

CLOSING DATE:

DATE:

PREVIOUS ADDRESS:

REALTOR

NAME:
AGENCY:
PHONE:
EMAIL:

CLOSING DATE:

DATE:

NOTES & REMINDERS

IMPORTANT *Contacts*

CLOSING ATTORNEY

NAME:

ADDRESS:

✉ EMAIL:

📞 PHONE:

MORTGAGE BROKER / COMPANY

NAME:

ADDRESS:

✉ EMAIL:

📞 PHONE:

MOVING COMPANY

NAME:

ADDRESS:

✉ EMAIL:

📞 PHONE:

HOME APPRAISER

NAME:

ADDRESS:

✉ EMAIL:

📞 PHONE:

NOTES & REMINDERS

IMPORTANT Dates

MONTH:

NOTES & REMINDERS

PROPERTY INSPECTION
Checklist

EXTERIOR CONDITION: GOOD   OK   BAD   **NOTES:**

EXTERIOR OF PROPERTY

FRONT DOOR

PORCH/DECK/PATIO

DRIVEWAY

GARAGE DOORS

OUTDOOR LIGHTING

PAINT & TRIM

WINDOWS

WALKWAY

ROOF CONDITION: GOOD   OK   BAD   **NOTES:**

CHIMNEY

GUTTERS & DOWNSPOUTS

SOFITS & FASCIA

YEAR ROOF WAS
REPLACED:

GARAGE CONDITION: GOOD   OK   BAD   **NOTES:**

CEILING

DOORS

FLOORS & WALLS

YEAR DOOR
OPENERS WERE
REPLACED:

YARD CONDITION: GOOD   OK   BAD   **NOTES:**

DRAINAGE

FENCES & GATES

RETAINING WALL

SPRINKLER SYSTEM

PROPERTY INSPECTION
Checklist

OTHER IMPORTANT AREAS: GOOD   OK   BAD   **NOTES:**

FOUNDATION

MASONRY VENEERS

EXTERIOR PAINT

STORM WINDOWS

PLUMBING

ELECTRICAL OUTLETS

FLOORING IN ROOMS

WOOD TRIM

FIREPLACE

KITCHEN CONDITION: GOOD   OK   BAD   **NOTES:**

WORKING EXHAUST FAN

NO LEAKS IN PIPES

APPLIANCES OPERATE

OTHER:

BATHROOM CONDITION: GOOD   OK   BAD   **NOTES:**

PROPER DRAINAGE

NO LEAKS IN PIPES

CAULKING IN GOOD SHAPE

TILES ARE SECURE

MISC: GOOD   OK   BAD   **NOTES:**

SMOKE & CARBON DETECTORS

STAIRWAY TREADS SOLID

STAIR HANDRAILS INSTALLED

OTHER:

OTHER:

OTHER:

HOUSE HUNTING *List*

PRICE	ADDRESS	NOTES

HOUSE HUNTING *List*

PRICE	ADDRESS	NOTES

HOUSE HUNTING *List*

PRICE	ADDRESS	NOTES

HOUSE HUNTING *List*

PRICE	ADDRESS	NOTES

HOUSE HUNTING *List*

PRICE	ADDRESS	NOTES

HOUSE HUNTING *List*

PRICE	ADDRESS	NOTES

HOUSE HUNTING *List*

PRICE	ADDRESS	NOTES

HOUSE HUNTING *List*

PRICE	ADDRESS	NOTES

HOUSE HUNTING *List*

PRICE	ADDRESS	NOTES

HOUSE HUNTING *List*

PRICE	ADDRESS	NOTES

HOUSE HUNTING *List*

PRICE	ADDRESS	NOTES

HOUSE HUNTING *List*

PRICE	ADDRESS	NOTES

HOUSE HUNTING
Checklist

HOUSE SCORE:

PROPERTY ADDRESS

ASKING PRICE: PROPERTY TAXES:

LOT SIZE: PROPERTY SIZE:

FINISH:
☐ BRICK   ☐ STUCCO
☐ WOOD   ☐ SIDING   AGE OF PROPERTY:

NEIGHBORHOOD

DISTANCE TO SCHOOLS: DISTANCE TO WORK:

PUBLIC TRANSPORTATION: MEDICAL:

RECREATION: SHOPPING:

ADDITIONAL INFO: NOTES:

HOUSE HUNTING *Checklist*

DETAILED HOUSE FEATURES:

OF BEDROOMS: # OF BATHROOMS:

BASEMENT: HEATING TYPE:

PROPERTY CHECKLIST:

				NOTES
POOL		BONUS ROOM		
GARAGE		LAUNDRY CHUTE		
FIREPLACE		FENCED YARD		
EN-SUITE		APPLIANCES		
OFFICE		A/C		
DECK		HEAT PUMP		

		NOTES
PARKING		
CLOSETS		
STORAGE		

HOUSE HUNTING
Checklist

HOUSE SCORE:

PROPERTY ADDRESS

ASKING PRICE:

PROPERTY TAXES:

LOT SIZE:

PROPERTY SIZE:

FINISH: ☐ BRICK ☐ STUCCO

☐ WOOD ☐ SIDING

AGE OF PROPERTY:

NEIGHBORHOOD

DISTANCE TO SCHOOLS:

DISTANCE TO WORK:

PUBLIC TRANSPORTATION:

MEDICAL:

RECREATION:

SHOPPING:

ADDITIONAL INFO:

NOTES:

HOUSE HUNTING *Checklist*

DETAILED HOUSE FEATURES:

OF BEDROOMS: # OF BATHROOMS:

BASEMENT: HEATING TYPE:

PROPERTY CHECKLIST:

POOL	☐	BONUS ROOM	☐	NOTES	
GARAGE	☐	LAUNDRY CHUTE	☐		
FIREPLACE	☐	FENCED YARD	☐		
EN-SUITE	☐	APPLIANCES	☐		
OFFICE	☐	A/C	☐		
DECK	☐	HEAT PUMP	☐		

PARKING	☐	NOTES
CLOSETS	☐	
STORAGE	☐	

HOUSE HUNTING
Checklist

HOUSE SCORE:

PROPERTY ADDRESS

ASKING PRICE:

PROPERTY TAXES:

LOT SIZE:

PROPERTY SIZE:

FINISH:
- [ ] BRICK
- [ ] STUCCO
- [ ] WOOD
- [ ] SIDING

AGE OF PROPERTY:

NEIGHBORHOOD

DISTANCE TO SCHOOLS:

DISTANCE TO WORK:

PUBLIC TRANSPORTATION:

MEDICAL:

RECREATION:

SHOPPING:

ADDITIONAL INFO:

NOTES:

HOUSE HUNTING *Checklist*

DETAILED HOUSE FEATURES:

OF BEDROOMS: # OF BATHROOMS:

BASEMENT: HEATING TYPE:

PROPERTY CHECKLIST:

POOL		BONUS ROOM		NOTES	
GARAGE		LAUNDRY CHUTE			
FIREPLACE		FENCED YARD			
EN-SUITE		APPLIANCES			
OFFICE		A/C			
DECK		HEAT PUMP			

PARKING		NOTES
CLOSETS		
STORAGE		

HOUSE HUNTING *Checklist*

DETAILED HOUSE FEATURES:

OF BEDROOMS: # OF BATHROOMS:

BASEMENT: HEATING TYPE:

PROPERTY CHECKLIST:

				NOTES
POOL		BONUS ROOM		
GARAGE		LAUNDRY CHUTE		
FIREPLACE		FENCED YARD		
EN-SUITE		APPLIANCES		
OFFICE		A/C		
DECK		HEAT PUMP		

		NOTES
PARKING		
CLOSETS		
STORAGE		

HOUSE HUNTING *Checklist*

DETAILED HOUSE FEATURES:

OF BEDROOMS:

OF BATHROOMS:

BASEMENT:

HEATING TYPE:

PROPERTY CHECKLIST:

POOL		BONUS ROOM		NOTES
GARAGE		LAUNDRY CHUTE		
FIREPLACE		FENCED YARD		
EN-SUITE		APPLIANCES		
OFFICE		A/C		
DECK		HEAT PUMP		

PARKING		NOTES
CLOSETS		
STORAGE		

HOUSE HUNTING
Checklist

HOUSE SCORE:

PROPERTY ADDRESS

ASKING PRICE:

PROPERTY TAXES:

LOT SIZE:

PROPERTY SIZE:

FINISH:
- [ ] BRICK
- [ ] STUCCO
- [ ] WOOD
- [ ] SIDING

AGE OF PROPERTY:

NEIGHBORHOOD

DISTANCE TO SCHOOLS:

DISTANCE TO WORK:

PUBLIC TRANSPORTATION:

MEDICAL:

RECREATION:

SHOPPING:

ADDITIONAL INFO:

NOTES:

HOUSE HUNTING *Checklist*

DETAILED HOUSE FEATURES:

OF BEDROOMS:

OF BATHROOMS:

BASEMENT:

HEATING TYPE:

PROPERTY CHECKLIST:

POOL		BONUS ROOM		NOTES
GARAGE		LAUNDRY CHUTE		
FIREPLACE		FENCED YARD		
EN-SUITE		APPLIANCES		
OFFICE		A/C		
DECK		HEAT PUMP		

PARKING		NOTES
CLOSETS		
STORAGE		

HOUSE HUNTING
Checklist

HOUSE SCORE:

PROPERTY ADDRESS

ASKING PRICE: PROPERTY TAXES:

LOT SIZE: PROPERTY SIZE:

FINISH: ☐ BRICK   ☐ STUCCO   AGE OF PROPERTY:
           ☐ WOOD   ☐ SIDING

NEIGHBORHOOD

DISTANCE TO SCHOOLS: DISTANCE TO WORK:

PUBLIC TRANSPORTATION: MEDICAL:

RECREATION: SHOPPING:

ADDITIONAL INFO: NOTES:

HOUSE HUNTING *Checklist*

DETAILED HOUSE FEATURES:

OF BEDROOMS: # OF BATHROOMS:

BASEMENT: HEATING TYPE:

PROPERTY CHECKLIST:

POOL	☐	BONUS ROOM	☐	NOTES	
GARAGE	☐	LAUNDRY CHUTE	☐		
FIREPLACE	☐	FENCED YARD	☐		
EN-SUITE	☐	APPLIANCES	☐		
OFFICE	☐	A/C	☐		
DECK	☐	HEAT PUMP	☐		

PARKING	☐	NOTES
CLOSETS	☐	
STORAGE	☐	
	☐	
	☐	
	☐	
	☐	
	☐	
	☐	
	☐	
	☐	
	☐	

HOUSE HUNTING *Checklist*

DETAILED HOUSE FEATURES:

OF BEDROOMS: # OF BATHROOMS:

BASEMENT: HEATING TYPE:

PROPERTY CHECKLIST:

				NOTES
POOL	☐	BONUS ROOM	☐	
GARAGE	☐	LAUNDRY CHUTE	☐	
FIREPLACE	☐	FENCED YARD	☐	
EN-SUITE	☐	APPLIANCES	☐	
OFFICE	☐	A/C	☐	
DECK	☐	HEAT PUMP	☐	

NOTES

PARKING	☐
CLOSETS	☐
STORAGE	☐

HOUSE HUNTING *Checklist*

DETAILED HOUSE FEATURES:

OF BEDROOMS: # OF BATHROOMS:

BASEMENT: HEATING TYPE:

PROPERTY CHECKLIST:

POOL		BONUS ROOM		NOTES
GARAGE		LAUNDRY CHUTE		
FIREPLACE		FENCED YARD		
EN-SUITE		APPLIANCES		
OFFICE		A/C		
DECK		HEAT PUMP		

PARKING		NOTES
CLOSETS		
STORAGE		

HOUSE HUNTING *Checklist*

DETAILED HOUSE FEATURES:

OF BEDROOMS: # OF BATHROOMS:

BASEMENT: HEATING TYPE:

PROPERTY CHECKLIST:

					NOTES
POOL		BONUS ROOM			
GARAGE		LAUNDRY CHUTE			
FIREPLACE		FENCED YARD			
EN-SUITE		APPLIANCES			
OFFICE		A/C			
DECK		HEAT PUMP			

		NOTES
PARKING		
CLOSETS		
STORAGE		

HOUSE HUNTING *Checklist*

DETAILED HOUSE FEATURES:

OF BEDROOMS: # OF BATHROOMS:

BASEMENT: HEATING TYPE:

PROPERTY CHECKLIST:

POOL		BONUS ROOM		NOTES
GARAGE		LAUNDRY CHUTE		
FIREPLACE		FENCED YARD		
EN-SUITE		APPLIANCES		
OFFICE		A/C		
DECK		HEAT PUMP		

PARKING		NOTES
CLOSETS		
STORAGE		

HOUSE HUNTING *Checklist*

DETAILED HOUSE FEATURES:

OF BEDROOMS: # OF BATHROOMS:

BASEMENT: HEATING TYPE:

PROPERTY CHECKLIST:

				NOTES
POOL	☐	BONUS ROOM	☐	
GARAGE	☐	LAUNDRY CHUTE	☐	
FIREPLACE	☐	FENCED YARD	☐	
EN-SUITE	☐	APPLIANCES	☐	
OFFICE	☐	A/C	☐	
DECK	☐	HEAT PUMP	☐	

NOTES

PARKING ☐

CLOSETS ☐

STORAGE ☐

☐

☐

☐

☐

☐

☐

☐

HOUSE HUNTING *Checklist*

DETAILED HOUSE FEATURES:

\# OF BEDROOMS: \# OF BATHROOMS:

BASEMENT: HEATING TYPE:

PROPERTY CHECKLIST:

				NOTES
POOL	☐	BONUS ROOM	☐	
GARAGE	☐	LAUNDRY CHUTE	☐	
FIREPLACE	☐	FENCED YARD	☐	
EN-SUITE	☐	APPLIANCES	☐	
OFFICE	☐	A/C	☐	
DECK	☐	HEAT PUMP	☐	

NOTES

PARKING	☐
CLOSETS	☐
STORAGE	☐
	☐
	☐
	☐
	☐
	☐
	☐
	☐
	☐

House Hunting NOTES

BUDGET & Expenses

PREVIOUS RESIDENCE

EXPENSES	BUDGET	ACTUAL	DIFFERENCE

NEW RESIDENCE

EXPENSES	BUDGET	ACTUAL	DIFFERENCE

OTHER

EXPENSES	BUDGET	ACTUAL	DIFFERENCE

BUDGET & *Expenses*

PREVIOUS RESIDENCE

EXPENSES	BUDGET	ACTUAL	DIFFERENCE

NEW RESIDENCE

EXPENSES	BUDGET	ACTUAL	DIFFERENCE

OTHER

EXPENSES	BUDGET	ACTUAL	DIFFERENCE

TO DO: *Previous Residence*

MOST IMPORTANT

NOTES:

TO DO: New Residence

MOST IMPORTANT

NOTES:

MOVING DAY *Planner*

PRIORITIES

MOVING DAY SCHEDULE

6 AM

7 AM

8 AM

9 AM

10 AM

MOVING DAY TO DO LIST

11 AM

12 PM

1 PM

2 PM

3 PM

4 PM

5 PM

6 PM

7 PM

8 PM

9 PM

10 PM

ORGANIZATION

11 PM

12 AM

REMINDERS

MOVING DAY *List*

OLD RESIDENCE	NEW RESIDENCE

MOVING DAY *List*

OLD RESIDENCE	NEW RESIDENCE

MOVING DAY *List*

Packing NOTES

ADDRESS CHANGE
Checklist

UTILITIES:

ELECTRIC

CABLE/SATELLITE

GAS

SECURITY SYSTEM

PHONE

INTERNET

WATER/SEWER

OTHER

OTHER

OTHER

FINANCIAL:

BANK

CREDIT CARD

BANK STATEMENTS

EMPLOYER

INSURANCE

OTHER

OTHER

OTHER

OTHER

OTHER

START/STOP *Utilities*

ELECTRIC COMPANY

NAME

PHONE

WEBSITE URL

START DATE

STOP DATE

ACCOUNT NUMBER

CABLE / SATELLITE

NAME

PHONE

WEBSITE URL

START DATE

STOP DATE

ACCOUNT NUMBER

GAS / HEATING COMPANY

NAME

PHONE

WEBSITE URL

START DATE

STOP DATE

ACCOUNT NUMBER

START/STOP *Utilities*

INTERNET PROVIDER

NAME

PHONE

WEBSITE URL

START DATE

STOP DATE

ACCOUNT NUMBER

SECURITY SYSTEM

NAME

PHONE

WEBSITE URL

START DATE

STOP DATE

ACCOUNT NUMBER

OTHER:

NAME

PHONE

WEBSITE URL

START DATE

STOP DATE

ACCOUNT NUMBER

NOTES:

NEW PROVIDER *Contacts*

MEDICAL

FAMILY DOCTOR

NAME:

PHONE:

EMAIL:

ADDRESS:

WEBSITE URL:

DENTIST

NAME:

PHONE:

EMAIL:

ADDRESS:

WEBSITE URL:

PEDIATRICIAN

NAME:

PHONE:

EMAIL:

ADDRESS:

WEBSITE URL:

NOTES

NEW PROVIDER *Contacts*

EDUCATION

SCHOOL #1:

NAME:

PHONE:

EMAIL:

ADDRESS:

WEBSITE URL:

SCHOOL #2:

NAME:

PHONE:

EMAIL:

ADDRESS:

WEBSITE URL:

SCHOOL #3:

NAME:

PHONE:

EMAIL:

ADDRESS:

WEBSITE URL:

NOTES

MOVING DAY *Planner*

6-WEEKS PRIOR

- [ ] HIRE A MOVING COMPANY
- [ ] KEEP RECEIPTS FOR TAX PURPOSES
- [ ] DETERMINE A BUDGET FOR MOVING EXPENSES
- [ ] ORGANIZE INVENTORY
- [ ] GET PACKING BOXES & LABELS
- [ ] PURGE / GIVE AWAY / SELL UNWANTED ITEMS
- [ ] CREATE AN INVENTORY SHEET OF ITEMS & BOXES
- [ ] RESEARCH SCHOOLS FOR YOUR CHILDREN
- [ ] PLAN A GARAGE SALE TO UNLOAD UNWANTED ITEMS

4-WEEKS PRIOR

- [ ] CONFIRM DATES WITH MOVING COMPANY
- [ ] RESEARCH YOUR NEW COMMUNITY
- [ ] START PACKING BOXES
- [ ] PURCHASE MOVING INSURANCE
- [ ] ORGANIZE FINANCIAL & LEGAL DOCUMENTS IN ONE PLACE
- [ ] FIND SNOW REMOVAL OR LANDSCAPE SERVICE FOR NEW RESIDENCE
- [ ] RESEARCH NEW DOCTOR, DENTIST, VETERNARIAN, ETC

2-WEEKS PRIOR

- [ ] PLAN FOR PET TRANSPORT DURING MOVE
- [ ] SET UP MAIL FORWARDING SERVICE
- [ ] TRANSFER HOMEOWNERS INSURANCE TO NEW RESIDENCE
- [ ] TRANSFER UTILITIES TO NEW RESIDENCE
- [ ] UPDATE YOUR DRIVER'S LICENSE

MOVING DAY *Planner*

6-WEEKS PRIOR

4-WEEKS PRIOR

2-WEEKS PRIOR

MOVING DAY *Planner*

WEEK OF MOVE

MOVING DAY

NOTES & REMINDERS

MOVING DAY *Planner*

6-WEEKS PRIOR

4-WEEKS PRIOR

2-WEEKS PRIOR

MOVING DAY *Planner*

WEEK OF MOVE

MOVING DAY

NOTES & REMINDERS

IMPORTANT DATES

Month

Notes

MOVING BOX *Inventory*

ROOM: BOX NO: COLOR CODE:

CONTENTS:

ROOM: BOX NO: COLOR CODE:

CONTENTS:

ROOM: BOX NO: COLOR CODE:

CONTENTS:

ROOM: BOX NO: COLOR CODE:

CONTENTS:

MOVING BOX *Inventory*

ROOM: BOX NO: COLOR CODE:

CONTENTS:

ROOM: BOX NO: COLOR CODE:

CONTENTS:

ROOM: BOX NO: COLOR CODE:

CONTENTS:

ROOM: BOX NO: COLOR CODE:

CONTENTS:

MOVING BOX *Inventory*

ROOM: BOX NO: COLOR CODE:

CONTENTS:

ROOM: BOX NO: COLOR CODE:

CONTENTS:

ROOM: BOX NO: COLOR CODE:

CONTENTS:

ROOM: BOX NO: COLOR CODE:

CONTENTS:

MOVING BOX *Inventory*

ROOM: BOX NO: COLOR CODE:

CONTENTS:

ROOM: BOX NO: COLOR CODE:

CONTENTS:

ROOM: BOX NO: COLOR CODE:

CONTENTS:

ROOM: BOX NO: COLOR CODE:

CONTENTS:

MOVING BOX *Inventory*

ROOM: BOX NO: COLOR CODE:

CONTENTS:

ROOM: BOX NO: COLOR CODE:

CONTENTS:

ROOM: BOX NO: COLOR CODE:

CONTENTS:

ROOM: BOX NO: COLOR CODE:

CONTENTS:

MOVING BOX *Inventory*

ROOM: BOX NO: COLOR CODE:

CONTENTS:

ROOM: BOX NO: COLOR CODE:

CONTENTS:

ROOM: BOX NO: COLOR CODE:

CONTENTS:

ROOM: BOX NO: COLOR CODE:

CONTENTS:

MOVING BOX *Inventory*

ROOM: **BOX NO:**   **COLOR CODE:**

CONTENTS:

ROOM: **BOX NO:**   **COLOR CODE:**

CONTENTS:

ROOM: **BOX NO:**   **COLOR CODE:**

CONTENTS:

ROOM: **BOX NO:**   **COLOR CODE:**

CONTENTS:

MOVING BOX *Inventory*

ROOM: BOX NO: COLOR CODE:

CONTENTS:

ROOM: BOX NO: COLOR CODE:

CONTENTS:

ROOM: BOX NO: COLOR CODE:

CONTENTS:

ROOM: BOX NO: COLOR CODE:

CONTENTS:

MOVING BOX *Inventory*

ROOM: BOX NO: COLOR CODE:

CONTENTS:

ROOM: BOX NO: COLOR CODE:

CONTENTS:

ROOM: BOX NO: COLOR CODE:

CONTENTS:

ROOM: BOX NO: COLOR CODE:

CONTENTS:

MOVING BOX *Inventory*

ROOM: BOX NO: COLOR CODE:

CONTENTS:

ROOM: BOX NO: COLOR CODE:

CONTENTS:

ROOM: BOX NO: COLOR CODE:

CONTENTS:

ROOM: BOX NO: COLOR CODE:

CONTENTS:

MOVING BOX *Inventory*

ROOM: BOX NO: COLOR CODE:

CONTENTS:

ROOM: BOX NO: COLOR CODE:

CONTENTS:

ROOM: BOX NO: COLOR CODE:

CONTENTS:

ROOM: BOX NO: COLOR CODE:

CONTENTS:

MOVING BOX *Inventory*

ROOM: BOX NO: COLOR CODE:

CONTENTS:

ROOM: BOX NO: COLOR CODE:

CONTENTS:

ROOM: BOX NO: COLOR CODE:

CONTENTS:

ROOM: BOX NO: COLOR CODE:

CONTENTS:

MOVING BOX *Inventory*

ROOM: BOX NO: COLOR CODE:

CONTENTS:

ROOM: BOX NO: COLOR CODE:

CONTENTS:

ROOM: BOX NO: COLOR CODE:

CONTENTS:

ROOM: BOX NO: COLOR CODE:

CONTENTS:

MOVING BOX *Inventory*

ROOM: BOX NO: COLOR CODE:

CONTENTS:

ROOM: BOX NO: COLOR CODE:

CONTENTS:

ROOM: BOX NO: COLOR CODE:

CONTENTS:

ROOM: BOX NO: COLOR CODE:

CONTENTS:

MOVING BOX *Inventory*

ROOM: BOX NO: COLOR CODE:

CONTENTS:

ROOM: BOX NO: COLOR CODE:

CONTENTS:

ROOM: BOX NO: COLOR CODE:

CONTENTS:

ROOM: BOX NO: COLOR CODE:

CONTENTS:

MOVING BOX *Inventory*

ROOM: BOX NO: COLOR CODE:

CONTENTS:

ROOM: BOX NO: COLOR CODE:

CONTENTS:

ROOM: BOX NO: COLOR CODE:

CONTENTS:

ROOM: BOX NO: COLOR CODE:

CONTENTS:

MOVING BOX *Inventory*

ROOM: BOX NO: COLOR CODE:

CONTENTS:

ROOM: BOX NO: COLOR CODE:

CONTENTS:

ROOM: BOX NO: COLOR CODE:

CONTENTS:

ROOM: BOX NO: COLOR CODE:

CONTENTS:

MOVING BOX *Inventory*

ROOM: BOX NO: COLOR CODE:

CONTENTS:

ROOM: BOX NO: COLOR CODE:

CONTENTS:

ROOM: BOX NO: COLOR CODE:

CONTENTS:

ROOM: BOX NO: COLOR CODE:

CONTENTS:

MOVING BOX *Inventory*

ROOM: BOX NO: COLOR CODE:

CONTENTS:

ROOM: BOX NO: COLOR CODE:

CONTENTS:

ROOM: BOX NO: COLOR CODE:

CONTENTS:

ROOM: BOX NO: COLOR CODE:

CONTENTS:

MOVING BOX *Inventory*

ROOM: BOX NO: COLOR CODE:

CONTENTS:

ROOM: BOX NO: COLOR CODE:

CONTENTS:

ROOM: BOX NO: COLOR CODE:

CONTENTS:

ROOM: BOX NO: COLOR CODE:

CONTENTS:

MOVING BOX *Inventory*

ROOM: BOX NO: COLOR CODE:

CONTENTS:

ROOM: BOX NO: COLOR CODE:

CONTENTS:

ROOM: BOX NO: COLOR CODE:

CONTENTS:

ROOM: BOX NO: COLOR CODE:

CONTENTS:

MOVING BOX *Inventory*

ROOM: BOX NO: COLOR CODE:

CONTENTS:

ROOM: BOX NO: COLOR CODE:

CONTENTS:

ROOM: BOX NO: COLOR CODE:

CONTENTS:

ROOM: BOX NO: COLOR CODE:

CONTENTS:

MOVING BOX *Inventory*

ROOM: BOX NO: COLOR CODE:

CONTENTS:

ROOM: BOX NO: COLOR CODE:

CONTENTS:

ROOM: BOX NO: COLOR CODE:

CONTENTS:

ROOM: BOX NO: COLOR CODE:

CONTENTS:

MOVING BOX *Inventory*

ROOM: BOX NO: COLOR CODE:

CONTENTS:

ROOM: BOX NO: COLOR CODE:

CONTENTS:

ROOM: BOX NO: COLOR CODE:

CONTENTS:

ROOM: BOX NO: COLOR CODE:

CONTENTS:

MOVING BOX *Inventory*

ROOM: BOX NO: COLOR CODE:

CONTENTS:

ROOM: BOX NO: COLOR CODE:

CONTENTS:

ROOM: BOX NO: COLOR CODE:

CONTENTS:

ROOM: BOX NO: COLOR CODE:

CONTENTS:

MOVING BOX *Inventory*

ROOM: BOX NO: COLOR CODE:

CONTENTS:

ROOM: BOX NO: COLOR CODE:

CONTENTS:

ROOM: BOX NO: COLOR CODE:

CONTENTS:

ROOM: BOX NO: COLOR CODE:

CONTENTS:

MOVING BOX *Inventory*

ROOM: BOX NO: COLOR CODE:

CONTENTS:

ROOM: BOX NO: COLOR CODE:

CONTENTS:

ROOM: BOX NO: COLOR CODE:

CONTENTS:

ROOM: BOX NO: COLOR CODE:

CONTENTS:

MOVING BOX *Inventory*

ROOM: BOX NO: COLOR CODE:

CONTENTS:

ROOM: BOX NO: COLOR CODE:

CONTENTS:

ROOM: BOX NO: COLOR CODE:

CONTENTS:

ROOM: BOX NO: COLOR CODE:

CONTENTS:

MOVING BOX *Inventory*

ROOM: BOX NO: COLOR CODE:

CONTENTS:

ROOM: BOX NO: COLOR CODE:

CONTENTS:

ROOM: BOX NO: COLOR CODE:

CONTENTS:

ROOM: BOX NO: COLOR CODE:

CONTENTS:

MOVING BOX *Inventory*

ROOM: BOX NO: COLOR CODE:

CONTENTS:

ROOM: BOX NO: COLOR CODE:

CONTENTS:

ROOM: BOX NO: COLOR CODE:

CONTENTS:

ROOM: BOX NO: COLOR CODE:

CONTENTS:

MOVING BOX *Inventory*

ROOM: BOX NO: COLOR CODE:

CONTENTS:

ROOM: BOX NO: COLOR CODE:

CONTENTS:

ROOM: BOX NO: COLOR CODE:

CONTENTS:

ROOM: BOX NO: COLOR CODE:

CONTENTS:

MOVING BOX *Inventory*

ROOM: BOX NO: COLOR CODE:

CONTENTS:

ROOM: BOX NO: COLOR CODE:

CONTENTS:

ROOM: BOX NO: COLOR CODE:

CONTENTS:

ROOM: BOX NO: COLOR CODE:

CONTENTS:

MOVING BOX *Inventory*

ROOM: BOX NO: COLOR CODE:

CONTENTS:

ROOM: BOX NO: COLOR CODE:

CONTENTS:

ROOM: BOX NO: COLOR CODE:

CONTENTS:

ROOM: BOX NO: COLOR CODE:

CONTENTS:

MOVING BOX *Inventory*

ROOM: BOX NO: COLOR CODE:

CONTENTS:

ROOM: BOX NO: COLOR CODE:

CONTENTS:

ROOM: BOX NO: COLOR CODE:

CONTENTS:

ROOM: BOX NO: COLOR CODE:

CONTENTS:

ROOM *Planner*

ROOM:

PAINT COLORS::

COLOR SCHEME:

DÉCOR IDEAS:

FURNITURE IDEAS:

NOTES:

ROOM:

PAINT COLORS::

COLOR SCHEME:

DÉCOR IDEAS:

FURNITURE IDEAS:

NOTES:

NEW ROOM *Planner*

ROOM:

PAINT COLORS:: ....

COLOR CODE: ....

DÉCOR IDEAS: ....

FURNITURE IDEAS: ....

THINGS TO DO:

- ☐ ....
- ☐ ....
- ☐ ....
- ☐ ....
- ☐ ....
- ☐ ....
- ☐ ....
- ☐ ....
- ☐ ....
- ☐ ....
- ☐ ....

DÉCOR IDEAS:

ROOM *Planner*

ROOM:

PAINT COLORS::

COLOR SCHEME:

DÉCOR IDEAS:

FURNITURE IDEAS:

NOTES:

ROOM:

PAINT COLORS::

COLOR SCHEME:

DÉCOR IDEAS:

FURNITURE IDEAS:

NOTES:

NEW ROOM *Planner*

ROOM:

PAINT COLORS::

COLOR CODE:

DÉCOR IDEAS:

FURNITURE IDEAS:

THINGS TO DO:

- [ ]
- [ ]
- [ ]
- [ ]
- [ ]
- [ ]
- [ ]
- [ ]
- [ ]
- [ ]
- [ ]

DÉCOR IDEAS:

ROOM *Planner*

ROOM:

PAINT COLORS::

COLOR SCHEME:

DÉCOR IDEAS:

FURNITURE IDEAS:

NOTES:

ROOM:

PAINT COLORS::

COLOR SCHEME:

DÉCOR IDEAS:

FURNITURE IDEAS:

NOTES:

NEW ROOM *Planner*

ROOM:

PAINT COLORS::

COLOR CODE:

DÉCOR IDEAS:

FURNITURE IDEAS:

THINGS TO DO:

- [ ]
- [ ]
- [ ]
- [ ]
- [ ]
- [ ]
- [ ]
- [ ]
- [ ]
- [ ]
- [ ]

DÉCOR IDEAS:

ROOM *Planner*

ROOM:

PAINT COLORS::

COLOR SCHEME:

DÉCOR IDEAS:

FURNITURE IDEAS:

NOTES:

ROOM:

PAINT COLORS::

COLOR SCHEME:

DÉCOR IDEAS:

FURNITURE IDEAS:

NOTES:

NEW ROOM *Planner*

ROOM:

PAINT COLORS::

COLOR CODE:

DÉCOR IDEAS:

FURNITURE IDEAS:

THINGS TO DO:

- [ ]
- [ ]
- [ ]
- [ ]
- [ ]
- [ ]
- [ ]
- [ ]
- [ ]
- [ ]
- [ ]

DÉCOR IDEAS:

ROOM *Planner*

ROOM:

PAINT COLORS::

COLOR SCHEME:

DÉCOR IDEAS:

FURNITURE IDEAS:

NOTES:

ROOM:

PAINT COLORS::

COLOR SCHEME:

DÉCOR IDEAS:

FURNITURE IDEAS:

NOTES:

NEW ROOM *Planner*

ROOM:

PAINT COLORS::

COLOR CODE:

DÉCOR IDEAS:

FURNITURE IDEAS:

THINGS TO DO:

- ☐
- ☐
- ☐
- ☐
- ☐
- ☐
- ☐
- ☐
- ☐
- ☐

DÉCOR IDEAS:

ROOM *Planner*

ROOM:

PAINT COLORS::

COLOR SCHEME:

DÉCOR IDEAS:

FURNITURE IDEAS:

NOTES:

ROOM:

PAINT COLORS::

COLOR SCHEME:

DÉCOR IDEAS:

FURNITURE IDEAS:

NOTES:

NEW ROOM *Planner*

ROOM:

PAINT COLORS::

COLOR CODE:

DÉCOR IDEAS:

FURNITURE IDEAS:

THINGS TO DO:

- [ ]
- [ ]
- [ ]
- [ ]
- [ ]
- [ ]
- [ ]
- [ ]
- [ ]
- [ ]
- [ ]

DÉCOR IDEAS:

ROOM *Planner*

ROOM:

PAINT COLORS::

COLOR SCHEME:

DÉCOR IDEAS:

FURNITURE IDEAS:

NOTES:

ROOM:

PAINT COLORS::

COLOR SCHEME:

DÉCOR IDEAS:

FURNITURE IDEAS:

NOTES:

NEW ROOM *Planner*

ROOM:

PAINT COLORS::

COLOR CODE:

DÉCOR IDEAS:

FURNITURE IDEAS:

THINGS TO DO:

- [ ]
- [ ]
- [ ]
- [ ]
- [ ]
- [ ]
- [ ]
- [ ]
- [ ]
- [ ]

DÉCOR IDEAS:

NEW ROOM *Planner*

ROOM:

PAINT COLORS::

COLOR CODE:

DÉCOR IDEAS:

FURNITURE IDEAS:

THINGS TO DO:

- [ ]
- [ ]
- [ ]
- [ ]
- [ ]
- [ ]
- [ ]
- [ ]
- [ ]
- [ ]
- [ ]

DÉCOR IDEAS:

NEW ROOM *Planner*

ROOM:

PAINT COLORS::

COLOR CODE:

DÉCOR IDEAS:

FURNITURE IDEAS:

THINGS TO DO:

- [ ] ....
- [ ] ....
- [ ] ....
- [ ] ....
- [ ] ....
- [ ] ....
- [ ] ....
- [ ] ....
- [ ] ....
- [ ] ....
- [ ] ....

DÉCOR IDEAS:

NEW ROOM *Planner*

ROOM:

PAINT COLORS::

COLOR CODE:

DÉCOR IDEAS:

FURNITURE IDEAS:

THINGS TO DO:

- [ ]
- [ ]
- [ ]
- [ ]
- [ ]
- [ ]
- [ ]
- [ ]
- [ ]
- [ ]
- [ ]

DÉCOR IDEAS:

NEW ROOM *Planner*

ROOM:

PAINT COLORS:: ....

COLOR CODE: ....

DÉCOR IDEAS: ....

FURNITURE IDEAS: ....

THINGS TO DO:

- [ ] ....
- [ ] ....
- [ ] ....
- [ ] ....
- [ ] ....
- [ ] ....
- [ ] ....
- [ ] ....
- [ ] ....
- [ ] ....

DÉCOR IDEAS:

ROOM *Planner*

ROOM:

PAINT COLORS::

COLOR SCHEME:

DÉCOR IDEAS:

FURNITURE IDEAS:

NOTES:

ROOM:

PAINT COLORS::

COLOR SCHEME:

DÉCOR IDEAS:

FURNITURE IDEAS:

NOTES:

NEW ROOM *Planner*

ROOM:

PAINT COLORS::

COLOR CODE:

DÉCOR IDEAS:

FURNITURE IDEAS:

THINGS TO DO:

- [ ]
- [ ]
- [ ]
- [ ]
- [ ]
- [ ]
- [ ]
- [ ]
- [ ]
- [ ]
- [ ]

DÉCOR IDEAS:

ROOM *Planner*

ROOM:

PAINT COLORS::

COLOR SCHEME:

DÉCOR IDEAS:

FURNITURE IDEAS:

NOTES:

ROOM:

PAINT COLORS::

COLOR SCHEME:

DÉCOR IDEAS:

FURNITURE IDEAS:

NOTES:

ROOM *Planner*

ROOM:

PAINT COLORS::

COLOR SCHEME:

DÉCOR IDEAS:

FURNITURE IDEAS:

NOTES:

ROOM:

PAINT COLORS::

COLOR SCHEME:

DÉCOR IDEAS:

FURNITURE IDEAS:

NOTES:

NEW ROOM *Planner*

ROOM:

PAINT COLORS::

COLOR CODE:

DÉCOR IDEAS:

FURNITURE IDEAS:

THINGS TO DO:

- [ ]
- [ ]
- [ ]
- [ ]
- [ ]
- [ ]
- [ ]
- [ ]
- [ ]
- [ ]
- [ ]

DÉCOR IDEAS:

NEW ROOM *Planner*

ROOM:

PAINT COLORS::

COLOR CODE:

DÉCOR IDEAS:

FURNITURE IDEAS:

THINGS TO DO:

- [ ]
- [ ]
- [ ]
- [ ]
- [ ]
- [ ]
- [ ]
- [ ]
- [ ]
- [ ]
- [ ]

DÉCOR IDEAS:

NEW ROOM *Planner*

ROOM:

PAINT COLORS::

COLOR CODE:

DÉCOR IDEAS:

FURNITURE IDEAS:

THINGS TO DO:

- [ ]
- [ ]
- [ ]
- [ ]
- [ ]
- [ ]
- [ ]
- [ ]
- [ ]
- [ ]
- [ ]

DÉCOR IDEAS:

ROOM *Planner*

ROOM:

PAINT COLORS::

COLOR SCHEME:

DÉCOR IDEAS:

FURNITURE IDEAS:

NOTES:

ROOM:

PAINT COLORS::

COLOR SCHEME:

DÉCOR IDEAS:

FURNITURE IDEAS:

NOTES:

NEW ROOM *Planner*

ROOM:

PAINT COLORS::
....

COLOR CODE:
....

DÉCOR IDEAS:
....

FURNITURE IDEAS:
....

THINGS TO DO:

- [ ] ....
- [ ] ....
- [ ] ....
- [ ] ....
- [ ] ....
- [ ] ....
- [ ] ....
- [ ] ....
- [ ] ....
- [ ] ....

DÉCOR IDEAS:

House Hunting NOTES